WORLD WAR II
WORLD WAR II IN EASTERN EUROPE

by Tristan Poehlmann

www.focusreaders.com

Copyright © 2023 by Focus Readers®, Lake Elmo, MN 55042. All rights reserved. No part of this book may be reproduced or utilized in any form or by any means without written permission from the publisher.

Focus Readers is distributed by North Star Editions:
sales@northstareditions.com | 888-417-0195

Produced for Focus Readers by Red Line Editorial.

Content Consultant: Dr. Gideon Mailer, Associate Professor of History, University of Minnesota Duluth

Photographs ©: Berliner Verlag/Archiv/Picture Alliance/DPA/AP Images, cover, 1, 26–27, 29; German War Department/AP Images, 4–5; Shutterstock, 7, 9, 13, 15, 16–17, 35, 37, 43; Library of Congress, 10–11; Naum Granovskiy/Sputnik/AP Images, 19; AP Images, 20–21, 25, 32–33, 39; Everett Collection Historical/Alamy, 23; HPR/AP Images, 31; CTK Photos/AP Images, 40–41; Red Line Editorial, 45

Library of Congress Cataloging-in-Publication Data
Names: Poehlmann, Tristan, author.
Title: World War II in Eastern Europe / by Tristan Poehlmann.
Description: Lake Elmo, MN : Focus Readers, [2023] | Series: World War II | Includes index. | Audience: Grades 4-6
Identifiers: LCCN 2022007157 (print) | LCCN 2022007158 (ebook) | ISBN 9781637392850 (hardcover) | ISBN 9781637393376 (paperback) | ISBN 9781637394359 (pdf) | ISBN 9781637393895 (ebook)
Subjects: LCSH: World War, 1939-1945--Europe, Eastern--Juvenile literature. | Europe, Eastern--History--1918-1945--Juvenile literature.
Classification: LCC D802.E92 P64 2023 (print) | LCC D802.E92 (ebook) | DDC 940.53/18--dc23/eng/20220216
LC record available at https://lccn.loc.gov/2022007157
LC ebook record available at https://lccn.loc.gov/2022007158

Printed in the United States of America
Mankato, MN
082022

ABOUT THE AUTHOR
Tristan Poehlmann is a freelance writer of educational nonfiction. A museum exhibit developer for many years, he also holds a master's degree in writing for children and young adults from Vermont College of Fine Arts. He lives in the San Francisco Bay Area.

TABLE OF CONTENTS

CHAPTER 1
An Unexpected Alliance 5

A CLOSER LOOK
Nazi Genocide 8

CHAPTER 2
Operation Barbarossa 11

CHAPTER 3
The Battle of Moscow 17

CHAPTER 4
The Siege of Leningrad 21

CHAPTER 5
The Battle of Stalingrad 27

CHAPTER 6
The Battle of Kursk 33

A CLOSER LOOK
Displaced Persons 38

CHAPTER 7
The Invasion of Germany 41

Focus on World War II in Eastern Europe • 46
Glossary • 47
To Learn More • 48
Index • 48

CHAPTER 1

AN UNEXPECTED ALLIANCE

In the summer of 1939, Nazi Germany and the Soviet Union stunned the world. The two nations announced the Molotov-Ribbentrop Pact. Germany and the Soviet Union promised that neither nation would attack the other.

Other countries in Europe had not expected this agreement. After all, the leaders of Germany and the Soviet Union disagreed strongly on political ideas. Adolf Hitler of Nazi Germany was

Representatives of Nazi Germany and the Soviet Union sign a pact on August 23, 1939.

a **fascist**. Joseph Stalin of the Soviet Union was a **Communist**. Their pact seemed strange.

Hitler and Stalin planned to take over Poland together. On September 1, 1939, Nazi Germany invaded western Poland. This event marked the beginning of World War II (1939–1945). Two weeks later, the Soviet Union took control of eastern Poland. Both armies crushed the Polish defenses. Hitler and Stalin split the nation in half. The Polish people were trapped under their violent control.

In response, Britain and France declared war on Germany. However, Hitler had an advantage in their fight. His Nazi political movement was already powerful. European leaders had allowed Nazi Germany to claim land in Austria and Czechoslovakia. Hitler's fascism and racism had gone unopposed for years.

Meanwhile, the Soviet Union continued to invade nations in Eastern Europe. People in all those places suffered. The war in Europe was spreading fast.

EASTERN EUROPE 1939–1940

A CLOSER LOOK

NAZI GENOCIDE

Hitler's racism was central to his political power. Nazi Germany used a racial status system that had no basis in reality. It supported Hitler's goal of destroying the Jewish people. Most European Jews lived in Eastern Europe. Invading that area was a key step in Hitler's plan.

The Nazis planned to claim the land for German settlers. They would colonize Eastern Europe. This matched an older idea called Lebensraum, or "living space." Lebensraum promised new land and natural resources to make Germany wealthy.

To Hitler, Lebensraum was a useful goal. It helped publicly justify the invasion of Poland. However, the main purpose of invading Eastern Europe was to carry out the **genocide** of Jews.

In Poland, Nazis forced Jews to live in crowded and deadly **ghettos**. From there, most Jews were sent to newly built death camps. Nazis used

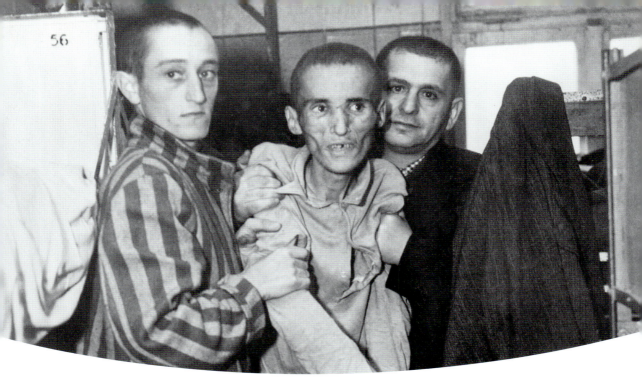

⚠ The Nazis murdered six million Jews during World War II. This event is known as the Holocaust.

the camps and ghettos to systematically kill millions of people. Only two percent of Polish Jews survived.

Nazis also carried out mass murder in the Soviet Union and beyond. As the Nazis invaded, they destroyed all Jewish communities. They shot men, women, and children and burned their houses. More than one million people died this way.

CHAPTER 2

OPERATION BARBAROSSA

Nazi Germany and the Soviet Union kept their pact for nearly two years. During that time, both nations got the land they wanted. However, Hitler and Stalin did not trust each other. Hitler did not plan to keep the pact forever. His racism and prejudice against Jews extended to the Soviet Union. Stalin had further plans as well. He wanted to gain control of a European port city. The two leaders' plans were in direct conflict.

In 1940, Stalin tried to negotiate new agreements with Nazi Germany.

Stalin and Hitler had very different political ideas. But at times, their goals were similar. Each leader wanted to build a totally pure society. They believed everyone in a pure society should think and act the same. They saw differences as a threat. Groups that did not fit their idea of perfection were considered enemies.

Nazi and Soviet leaders used extreme violence against those groups. Stalin killed people who had political differences. Hitler did the same. But Hitler went much further. He specifically targeted Europe's large Jewish population.

In 1940, Nazi Germany invaded much of Western Europe. However, Hitler believed those nations were similar to Germany. Their major **ethnic groups** fit his false idea of racial superiority. In contrast, Eastern European ethnic groups did not fit that idea. For example, Hitler

▲ German soldiers reached the Soviet city of Minsk a few days after launching Operation Barbarossa.

saw Slavic people as inferior. But he thought they could be useful laborers. However, Hitler did not see Jews as human at all.

Hitler broke the Molotov-Ribbentrop Pact in June 1941. That month, Nazi Germany launched a surprise attack on the Soviet Union. The plan was code-named Operation Barbarossa. It was the largest invasion in history. The Soviet army was not ready for it. The invasion created a massive new Eastern Front of the war.

The Eastern Front was a deadly place. Soviet soldiers fought furiously to guard their land and people. By September, more than two million Soviet soldiers were dead or wounded. The Nazis seized food as they moved across the land. Soldiers fed themselves and starved the people who lived there. This was part of a strategy called the Hunger Plan.

The invasion destroyed communities of Jews, Roma, and other people. Death squads rounded up the Jews living in each town. Locals often betrayed their Jewish neighbors. Whole

➤ CONSIDER THIS

People in Eastern Europe experienced the war very differently than most people in Western Europe. What were some of the causes of this?

▲ German soldiers lead Polish women into a forest to kill them.

families were shot in organized mass killings. In some areas, locals carried out these mass murders themselves.

By late 1941, Nazi Germany was at the height of its power. Hitler had control over the majority of European nations. Finally, in December of that year, the United States entered the war.

CHAPTER 3

THE BATTLE OF MOSCOW

Nazi Germany attacked the Soviet Union from three separate national borders. Armies invaded from Finland, Poland, and Romania. They planned to surround the Soviet troops. Within a few weeks, parts of the Soviet border had been pushed back hundreds of miles. Germany expected a quick victory.

The Soviet Union desperately needed allies. Stalin allowed talks between Soviet and British

Soviet tanks burn during Nazi Germany's 1941 invasion.

politicians. Stalin did not trust the British. He thought they might sign a pact with Germany. But he had not expected Hitler's invasion. As a result, the Soviet Union was low on defenses.

By the late summer of 1941, the Soviet army was getting stronger. Even so, it had already lost vast areas of land. Nazi troops had burned numerous towns and murdered the people living there. However, their invasion was taking longer than planned. By the time they reached the Soviet capital of Moscow, it was almost winter.

Moscow had spent months preparing for the invasion. The battle began with fierce fighting along the roads. But the German army was low on supplies. As Nazi soldiers pushed farther into the Soviet Union, fewer supplies could reach them. The soldiers were hungry and cold. Many of their tanks were stuck in the snow. Action slowed.

▲ In late 1941, many streets in Moscow were filled with barricades to prevent the German army from advancing.

It was a harsh winter for everyone. The Soviet army also struggled. Snow blocked the roads out of Moscow. Travel was dangerous. The battle was long and miserable. But slowly, Soviet soldiers took back the city's suburbs. Eventually, the Nazis began to retreat from Moscow.

The Soviets had won the battle. They had also gained Britain and the United States as allies.

CHAPTER 4

THE SIEGE OF LENINGRAD

As 1941 progressed, Hitler's attention moved toward the Soviet economy. He wanted to stop the Soviet Union's ability to produce weapons. One of his main targets was the city of Leningrad. The factories in Leningrad were busy producing engines, tanks, and guns. Hitler knew the Soviet army could not fight for long without this new equipment.

A Soviet worker packs ammunition into a case so that it can be sent to the army.

The Nazis planned to destroy Leningrad and its people. The city lay near the border with Finland. So, Nazi Germany made a land deal with Finland in return for help. The two armies would surround Leningrad. They would block all supply lines. Without food, the city would have to surrender.

The German and Finnish armies approached Leningrad in September 1941. They took control of roads and railroad lines. There was no way to get into or out of the city. For weeks, Leningrad was shelled and bombed. The city of three million people only had enough food to survive for one month. But the **Siege** of Leningrad did not fully end for more than three years.

The autumn of 1941 was just the beginning of the hard times. Soviet soldiers held a line around the city. Groups of volunteers built layers of defenses. Women and children dug ditches and

▲ Soviet citizens dig ditches around the city of Leningrad to stop German tanks.

cut down trees. They set up barbed-wire fences. Others built concrete shelters. Volunteers in the city fought huge fires caused by the bombing.

By November, the people in Leningrad were starving. Food was scarce. People survived on moldy bread with jelly made from sheep guts. They made soup out of glue or Vaseline. Fuel was also low. People walked miles to work or school. They slept in dark, cold homes. Each day, thousands of people died of starvation.

The winter was even more difficult. Until February 1942, supplies were very low. Several months earlier, the Soviets had built a small port on a nearby lake. However, the German army had fired on the supply boats. Once the lake froze, it became somewhat safer. Small trucks could drive across with supplies. The ice was so thick that most Nazi shells only made potholes. Trucks full of supplies kept Leningrad's people alive. But the siege continued.

It took another two years before Leningrad was freed. The German army did not retreat until January 1944. By that point, the city had been

> **CONSIDER THIS**

Some historians have called the Siege of Leningrad a genocide. Do you agree? Why or why not?

▲ People flee from their burning homes during the Siege of Leningrad.

bombed into ruins. Approximately one million people had died. Most of them starved to death.

During the years that Leningrad was under siege, Nazi Germany also held control of Paris, France. However, the outcome there was vastly different. In Paris, there was very little bombing and far less death. Hitler wanted to rule the people of Paris. In Leningrad, he wanted to kill people.

CHAPTER 5

THE BATTLE OF STALINGRAD

In the summer of 1942, Nazi Germany found a new point of invasion. Nazi soldiers quickly took over the area between the Black Sea and the Caspian Sea. The Soviet defense got off to a bad start. The disorganized soldiers soon retreated in confusion. Defeat now seemed close.

This shock led to a sudden change in the national mood. Stalin declared that soldiers who did not show discipline would be shot. And many

German soldiers move through the Black Sea region of the Soviet Union.

27

were. Meanwhile, fear for the survival of the nation fed people's anger. Newspapers, plays, and poems called for brutal violence against Germany. Many Soviet people expressed intense hatred. They wanted the German army totally destroyed.

The new Nazi attack had a practical purpose. Germany needed more oil. The invasion of the Soviet Union had lasted longer than planned. The Nazis could not keep going without a fuel source. Hitler wanted to control the oil fields by the Caspian Sea. The German army could get there using the Volga River. So, soldiers moved toward Stalingrad, a key city along the Volga.

The Soviet army's rapid retreat had given Hitler confidence. As the Soviets fled, Hitler changed his plan of attack. He split up the German troops. One group would stay on track to Stalingrad. The other group would head straight for the oil fields.

▲ Huge clouds of smoke rise into the air after German planes bomb Stalingrad.

Hitler believed two battles could be fought and won at the same time.

By August, Nazi troops neared Stalingrad. Their first attack was a massive bombing raid. Fires burned the city for miles as buildings collapsed.

Before the German soldiers even entered Stalingrad, they had killed thousands of the city's people. Hitler's orders targeted both **civilians** and soldiers. Everyone who remained in the city fought in the Battle of Stalingrad.

German tanks rolled into the city center in September. Their goal was to win control of the Volga River and the factories. For months, fighting moved back and forth on foot, street by street. Soviet soldiers hid in the bombed-out buildings. They fought to hold each sidewalk and step.

Winter came. Everyone in Stalingrad was tired, hungry, and cold. The temperature dropped far below freezing. However, the Soviet army was slowly winning. By January, Nazi troops were surrounded and stuck. After more than four months of miserable fighting, the German army surrendered.

⚞ Captured German soldiers walk through the ruins of Stalingrad in early 1943.

For the Eastern Front and for the world, this moment was a turning point. Nazi Germany had taken thousands of square miles of land. Its army had killed millions of people. The Nazis seemed unstoppable. Now, with a massive empire in their grasp, they had lost. Hitler's army was in retreat.

CHAPTER 6

THE BATTLE OF KURSK

Victory at Stalingrad changed how Western European leaders viewed the Soviet Union. They began to see the country as strong. This shift put the Soviet Union on a path to international power. But at the time, the victory mainly lifted the Soviet people's confidence. Their army was still far from defeating the Nazi forces.

In May 1943, a new battle was brewing. The city of Kursk lay south of Moscow and west of

Soviet soldiers achieved an important victory at the Battle of Stalingrad.

33

Stalingrad. It was an important railroad hub. Hitler wanted to capture the city and have his army head straight for Moscow. But Stalin had been informed about this plan in advance. A **resistance** group alerted the British government. The Soviet army was prepared.

Outside of Kursk, towns had been evacuated that spring. People worked to build a defense system around the city. They spent months digging ditches and creating barriers. Six rings of defenses spread hundreds of miles across the region. Supplies from the Allied nations also began arriving that spring. The Soviet army gained thousands of American and British tanks, trucks, and airplanes.

The German army also worked quickly to prepare for battle. New tanks and weapons were moved by train and set into position.

▲ Soviet workers built tanks around the clock at factories near the Ural Mountains.

Hitler planned a massive show of force. He wanted to show that Nazi Germany was not on the defensive. But he also had doubts about the attack. He did not want to repeat the mistakes of Stalingrad.

The Battle of Kursk was the largest tank battle in history. These moving fortresses were powerful weapons. The Nazis used tanks as spearheads. They rammed into the Soviet army's lines while firing on them. In defense, the Soviets used their tanks to make an obstacle course while firing back.

Only airplanes could drop bombs that destroyed tanks. As a result, Soviet troops on the ground could rarely damage German tanks. Skilled sharpshooters could target a tank pilot by aiming at the tank's viewing slit. But it was a difficult shot.

The battle's key moments took place over several days in July. Nazi tanks tried to surround and cut off Soviet troops. However, their own movements slowed when they hit Soviet minefields. Shelling and bombing destroyed

▲ The Panzer 38(t) was one variety of tank used by Nazi Germany throughout the war.

many German tanks. Thick mud and mechanical problems slowed others.

Seeing this situation, many Nazis started to retreat right away. Some of the troop positions were held until September. But the Soviet Union had clearly won the Battle of Kursk. In the fall of 1943, the Soviet army pushed the German forces back to where they had been in 1941. The power balance on the Eastern Front had changed for the last time.

A CLOSER LOOK

DISPLACED PERSONS

Civilians in Eastern Europe suffered terribly during the war. People were sent to **labor camps**, concentration camps, and prisons. Those who survived often lost their homes, belongings, or communities. After the war, they were called displaced persons (DPs).

Approximately eight million people in Europe were considered DPs. Most were resettled in some way within a few months. Still, more than one million DPs had nowhere to go. This included 250,000 Jews. Many had fled the Nazi invasion of Eastern Europe. During the war, they struggled to survive in hiding. When the war ended, everything they once had was gone.

Emigration was a common way to start over. However, it was not always possible. Most nations allowed only small numbers of immigrants.

▲ British soldiers stand guard over a DP camp where Jews live in simple shacks.

For example, the United States passed laws that limited Jewish immigrants.

Instead, DP camps were set up as temporary refugee housing. The camps were crowded and often unsafe. Genocide survivors suffered further violence. Food and clothing were scarce. Many people waited for years before they could emigrate. Ultimately, most Jewish DPs moved to Palestine, Israel, the United States, Canada, or Australia.

CHAPTER 7

THE INVASION OF GERMANY

By May 1944, the Soviet Union had taken back most of its land from Nazi Germany. However, Stalin still wanted to control more of Eastern Europe. His goal happened to fit into the Soviet army's new role.

The Allied nations planned to invade Nazi Germany from two sides. Britain and France would attack from the west. At the same time, the Soviet army would keep pushing from the east.

Allied military leaders make plans on the Eastern Front in 1944.

Resistance groups in Nazi-occupied areas were also at work. Eastern European resistance groups were highly effective against the German army. They derailed supply trains. They set off explosives that blew up train tracks and bridges. All of these actions slowed Nazi communications.

Many Jews fought in the resistance. They escaped mass murders, ghettos, or camps and lived deep inside forests. They armed themselves and connected to resistance groups. One large group of 1,000 Jews survived the war hidden in a remote forest swamp. They destroyed train tracks and assisted in escapes from ghettos.

Soviet troops took over much of Eastern Europe in the spring of 1944. They saw evidence of genocide. Mass graves held entire Jewish communities that had been murdered together. Slavic prisoners of war and civilians

▲ Nazis murdered approximately one million Jews at the Auschwitz death camp.

had died of starvation and forced labor. As the Nazis retreated, they had burned down hundreds of towns.

The Soviet army moved quickly through a nearly empty landscape. Few people had survived. Even the cities were destroyed. By fall, the army was in eastern Poland. Troops soon found evidence of a death camp. Jews and other groups had been murdered there on a massive scale.

It was so shocking that international newspapers did not believe the report. But as the Soviet army continued, it liberated camps where people were still alive to tell the truth.

By the spring of 1945, the Allied armies were positioned to invade Nazi Germany. The Soviet army would take control of Berlin, the German capital. Troops surrounded the city. Heavy fighting brought them through the suburbs. The battle was vicious and destructive. Soviet troops attacked and killed German civilians along with soldiers.

As Soviet troops neared central Berlin, Hitler took his own life. Within days, Berlin was under Soviet control. On May 9, 1945, Nazi Germany officially surrendered to the Soviet army.

World War II claimed more lives than any other war in history. The events in Eastern Europe are not always familiar to people in Western nations. But Eastern Europe was the center of World War II's conflict and killing.

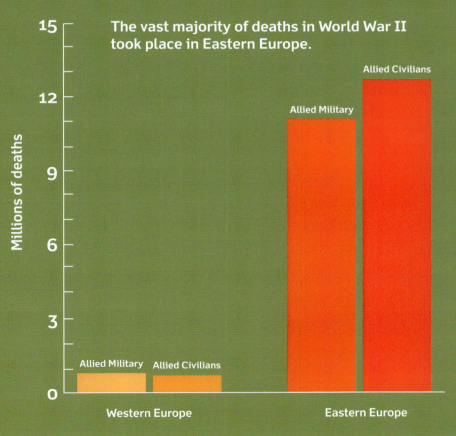

FOCUS ON
WORLD WAR II IN EASTERN EUROPE

Write your answers on a separate piece of paper.

1. Write a paragraph that explains what happened to Eastern European Jews during World War II.

2. Based on what you read about fighting on the Eastern Front, do you think a strong attack or a strong defense is more important for winning a battle? Why?

3. How many civilians died of starvation during the Siege of Leningrad?

    A. one million
    B. two million
    C. three million

4. At the Battle of Kursk, the German army tried not to repeat its mistake from the Battle of Stalingrad. What was that mistake?

    A. They bombed the city before entering.
    B. They had no way to retreat.
    C. They attacked in tanks instead of on foot.

Answer key on page 48.

GLOSSARY

civilians
People who are not in the military.

Communist
Someone who belongs to a political party that believes the government should own all property.

emigration
The act of moving to a different country.

ethnic groups
Groups of people who share the same culture, language, or place of origin.

fascist
Someone who believes a country should be led by a strong ruler and that violence should be used to silence opposing groups.

genocide
The act of killing a large number of people from a specific nation or ethnic group.

ghettos
Parts of cities, often closed off by walls or fences, that limit the movement of minority groups.

labor camps
Prisons where people are forced to do difficult work.

resistance
A secret group that fights against an occupying enemy force.

siege
An attack in which soldiers surround a town or other area and cut off all its supplies in an attempt to force it to surrender.

TO LEARN MORE

BOOKS

Batalion, Judy. *The Light of Days (Young Readers' Edition): The Untold Story of Women Resistance Fighters in Hitler's Ghettos*. New York: HarperCollins, 2020.

Shulevitz, Uri. *Chance: Escape from the Holocaust*. New York: Farrar, Straus and Giroux, 2020.

Wein, Elizabeth. *A Thousand Sisters: The Heroic Airwomen of the Soviet Union in World War II*. New York: HarperCollins, 2019.

NOTE TO EDUCATORS

Visit **www.focusreaders.com** to find lesson plans, activities, links, and other resources related to this title.

INDEX

Britain, 6, 19, 41

displaced persons, 38–39

France, 6, 25, 41

genocide, 8, 24, 39, 42

Hitler, Adolf, 5–6, 8, 11–13, 15, 18, 21, 25, 28–31, 34–35, 44

Jews, 8–9, 11–14, 38–39, 42–43

Kursk, Battle of, 33–37

Leningrad, Siege of, 21–25

Moscow, Battle of, 17–19

Poland, 6, 8, 17, 43

resistance groups, 34, 42

Stalin, Joseph, 6, 11–12, 17–18, 27, 34, 41

Stalingrad, Battle of, 27–31

United States, 15, 19, 39

Answer Key: 1. Answers will vary; 2. Answers will vary; 3. A; 4. B